P

1

PORTRAIT OF
LEICESTERSHIRE
& RUTLAND

GRAHAM OLIVER

HALSGROVE

DEDICATION

To my Mum and Dad

First published in Great Britain in 2010

British Library Cataloguing-in-Publication Data
A CIP record for this title is available from the British Library

ISBN 978 1 84114 994 3

HALSGROVE
Halsgrove House,
Ryelands Industrial Estate,
Bagley Road, Wellington, Somerset TA21 9PZ
Tel: 01823 653777   Fax: 01823 216796
email: sales@halsgrove.com

Part of the Halsgrove group of companies
Information on all Halsgrove titles is available at: www.halsgrove.com

Printed and bound in China by Toppan Leefung Printing Ltd

INTRODUCTION

The aim of this book is to capture not only the well known tourist attractions but also the less familiar corners of both Leicestershire and Rutland. Although often linked together, Leicestershire and Rutland are in fact two separate counties as Rutland once again was awarded county status in 1997.

Neither county has a coastline nor any rugged, mountain scenery but Leicestershire and Rutland are able to make many boasts. The Great Central Railway which runs from Loughborough to Leicester North is the only double track, main line heritage railway in the UK. Rutland water, a reservoir the size of Lake Windermere, is one of the biggest man-made lakes in Europe. The National Space Centre, situated on the banks of the River Soar in Leicester, is the Uks' largest attraction dedicated to space. Foxton Locks on the Grand Union Canal is one of the longest flights of staircase locks in England. The Battle of Bosworth in August 1485 was one of the most influential battles fought on English soil. And Leicesters' Diwali celebrations on Belgrave Road are the largest in the world outside India.

Leicestershire and Rutland are predominantly a landscape of rolling green farmland with some areas of higher ground, notably the Charnwood Forest area around Beacon Hill and parts of the newly formed National Forest around Coalville. The highest summit in the area is Bardon Hill overlooking Coalville at 278 metres (912 feet) Many locals, including myself before embarking on this book, assumed Beacon Hill was the highest spot in Leicestershire but the rocky crags of this country park only manage 248 metres (815 feet)

Other high spots include Burrough-on-the-Hill to the south of Melton Mowbray and the area around Waltham on the Wolds to the north of Melton Mowbray. Croft Hill commands spectacular views of South Leicestershire and the city of Leicester can be seen to the north. Both Croft Hill and Bardon Hill have been dramatically gouged away by the quarrying industry.

In terms of their shape, Leicestershire and Rutland together are roughly circular on the pages of a map with the city of Leicester a focal point in the middle. The road network converges on the city from all points of the compass, splitting the area into segments like it is an orange.

The industrial heritage of the area is evident in the factories of Leicester and the larger towns which were built to serve the hosiery, knitwear and footwear industries. Engineering has also been an important industry and evidence of heavier industries can be found in northwest Leicestershire. Snibston Colliery still stands at Snibston Discovery Park in Coalville and Moira Furnace is now a museum on the Ashby Canal. Both the Ashby Canal and the Grand Union Canal played an important role in the region's industrial past.

Jewry Wall is the oldest building in Leicester dating back to roman times and overlooking the ruins of the city's roman baths. One of the most iconic buildings in the two counties is Belvoir Castle which commands a spectacular position overlooking the Vale of Belvoir. Another splendid, historical landmark is Kirby Muxloe Castle which remained unfinished because the person building it, Lord Hastings, was executed for treason by Richard III. The county didn't afford the king much luck either because he was killed at the Battle of Bosworth.

Other historic monuments include Ashby Castle, Oakham Castle and the ruins of Bradgate House in Bradgate Park which was the home of Lady Jane Grey, the Nine Days Queen, who was also executed.

If you live in Leicestershire and Rutland, I hope you can identify and enjoy a photo near where you live. Perhaps these photos will encourage you to explore new places. If you live outside the two counties, I hope this book will inspire you to visit.

Kirby Muxloe Castle
The castle is actually an unfinished, fortified manor house. Work was begun in 1480 by
William Hastings but was never completed after Hastings was executed for treason by Richard III in 1483.

St Peter's Church, Gaulby
The pinnacles on top of the tower are the distinctive feature of this rural church.

Barrowden, Rutland
The duck pond and village green provide an idyllic setting for the Exeter Arms public house.

Grace Dieu Priory
The priory is an Augustinian nunnery dating from circa 1235. The ruins are preserved by the Grace Dieu Priory Trust.

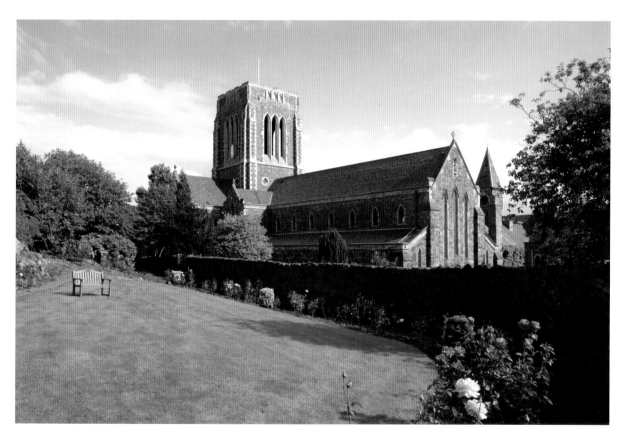

Mount Saint Bernard Abbey
The abbey is a Cistercian Monastery of the Strict Observance, founded in 1835.

Somerby
The Stilton Cheese Inn on a beautiful August morning.

Burrough on the Hill Country Park
One of the highest points in Leicestershire at 690 feet (210 metres)
The hill is crowned by an Iron Age fort with well preserved ramparts.

Walton
This chalet-style cottage
is now a farm shop and
used to be a pub.

Walkers Stadium, Leicester
The stadium has been the home of Leicester City Football Club since 2002.

Newton Linford
Evening descends on All Saints Church which is at the entrance to Bradgate Park.

Bradgate Park
Deer graze in the idyllic surroundings of Leicester's largest and most popular Country Park.

Shackerstone
Autumn colours reflected in the Ashby Canal at Shackerstone.

Ambion Wood
The trail which leads through Ambion Wood connecting the
Ashby Canal at Sutton Cheney to the Bosworth Battlefield.

Rutland Street, Leicester
The modern architecture of the new Curve Theatre contrasts with the existing buildings on Rutland Street.

Leicester Clock Tower
Constructed in 1868, this famous Leicester landmark depicts the statues of these eminent Leicester citizens: Simon de Montfort, William Wyggeston, Thomas White and Gabriel Newton.

Peatling Magna
All Saints Church is surrounded by green fields on the edge of the village.

Shearsby
The village green and St Mary Magdalene Church on an autumn afternoon.

Seagrave
Seagrave was the recent winner of the 'Leicestershire Village of the Year' in a national competition.

Sileby
Narrowboats moored on the River Soar at Sileby Mill with the village of Sileby in the distance.

St Giles church, Blaston
Tree trunks and sheep add to the rural setting of St Giles church.

Straw bales near Slawston
A circular straw bale stands out against a stormy sky near the village of Slawston.

Bradgate House in Bradgate Park
An old oak tree frames the ruins of Bradgate House, the birthplace of Lady Jane Grey, the Nine Days Queen.

Broughton Astley
The half-timbered façade of the Ye Olde Bulls Head pub hides under the canopy of a large weeping willow.

Market Bosworth
Market Bosworth can be seen in the distance from the path around the Bosworth Battlefield.

Almshouses, Appleby Magna
These cottages were built in 1839 to provide accommodation for the poor people of the parish.

St Peter's Church, Empingham, Rutland
This village is situated on the northern shore of Rutland Water close to the dam.

Belvoir Castle

The ancestral home of the Duke and Duchess of Rutland, Belvoir Castle is one of Leicestershire's most prominent landmarks. For more information visit www.belvoircastle.com

Use of this photo by kind permission of His Grace The Duke of Rutland. © The Duke of Rutland 2009

The National Space Centre, Leicester
The futuristic rocket tower of the UK's largest attraction dedicated to space.
A reflection of the tower is distorted by a gentle ripple on the River Soar.

Southfields Library, Leicester
Southfields Library on Saffron Lane is better known as the
'Pork Pie Library' because of its distinctive circular shape.

St Deny's Church, Ibstock
The town of Ibstock in north-west Leicestershire is situated within the National Forest.

Ashby de la Zouch Castle
The addition of the words 'de la Zouch' date back to the Norman Conquest when a Norman nobleman inherited the town.
The castle was used in a scene by Walter Scott for his novel *Ivanhoe* and is now maintained by English Heritage.

Bradgate Park
A knotted tree catches the sunlight in Bradgate Park. The folly of Old John,
an iconic Leicestershire landmark, is just visible on the hill.

Bradgate House and Chapel, Bradgate Park

Golden autumn leaves lead the eye towards Bradgate Chapel and the ruins of Bradgate House.

Diwali, Belgrave Road, Leicester
Diwali illuminations on Belgrave Road. Diwali is the Hindu Festival of Light
and the celebrations in Leicester are the largest in the world outside India.

Diwali lights and traffic trails, Belgrave Road, Leicester
Using a long exposure of ten seconds, in this instance, causes the brake lights and
indicators of passing traffic to be recorded as colourful streaks of light.

The Leicestershire Fox
The fox is Leicestershire's mascot as well as being the mascot for Leicester City Football Club.
The county's association with the fox is due to its tradition of fox hunting.

The Rutting Season, Bradgate Park
A Red Deer stag lifts back its head and roars like a lion.

The Ashby Canal at Shackerstone
The Ashby Canal curves into the distance and provides narrowboats with permanent moorings.

St Andrew's Church, Lyddington, Rutland

Like many of the buildings in the village, this sturdy looking church was built out of local ironstone. The church is situated next to Bede House, a medieval palace which belonged to the Bishops of Lincoln.

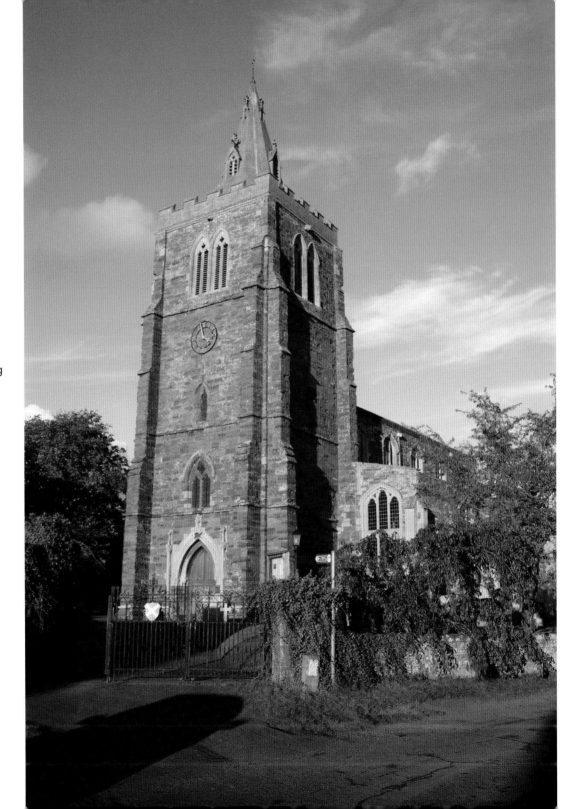

St Dionysius Church, Market Harborough
December sunlight casts a strong shadow over the roman numerals of the
sundial located on the tower of the main church in Market Harborough.

Barrow upon Soar
The Navigation public house and a bridge over the River Soar on a cold December morning.

St John the Baptist Church, Kings Norton
This famous Leicestershire church can be seen for miles around. A spire was added to the tower in 1775 but was destroyed by lightning in 1850.

The Great Central Railway, Loughborough
The G.C.R. is Britain's only mainline heritage railway. Here a Santa Special bellows out steam as it pulls away from Loughborough Central Station.

Foxton Locks

A heavy frost adds a seasonal touch to one of Leicestershire's most popular tourist attractions. Foxton Locks comprise of two 'staircases' of five consecutive locks enabling the Grand Union Canal to climb a steep hill.

The Grand Union Canal, Foxton
The canal is partially frozen on a bitterly cold December morning.
My car thermometer recorded a temperature of minus six!

Town Hall Square, Leicester
Old fashioned lamps and Christmas lights illuminate Town Hall Square at dusk.

Town Hall Square Fountain, Leicester
The ornamental fountain, featuring bronze painted lions, was donated to Leicester Council in 1878 by Israel Hart, a former mayor.

Oakham
The tower and spire of All Saints Church enhance the location of Oakham Castle.

Oakham Castle
All that remains of Oakham Castle today is the Great Hall which dates back to
the twelfth century. The castle is open to the public and is licensed to hold weddings.

Ayston, Rutland
A snow covered farm track and St Mary the Virgin Church create a
Christmas card scene at this quiet village just north of Uppingham. I used to love
snow as a child and I felt a great sense of nostalgia as I stood taking this photo.

Burton Overy
The road between Burton Overy and Carlton Curlieu covered by a light fall of
snow on a beautiful January morning. Taking the photos for this book coincided with the
whitest winter in Leicestershire and Rutland for eighteen years so there are a number of snow scenes!

Croft Hill

Croft Hill overlooks one of the largest granite quarries in Europe. The side of
the quarry can be seen behind the trig point. The village of Huncote can be seen in
the middle distance and the city of Leicester is distinguishable just below the horizon.

St Mary's Church, Melton Mowbray
The church dates from 1170 and the hundred foot tower is a dominant feature in the town. I still go
to the dentist in Melton Mowbray and this image was taken when I was early for an appointment.
Taking photos seemed a better alternative than sitting in a dentist's waiting room!

Uppingham, Rutland
Traditional stone buildings add character to this old market town.

Uppingham School
A statue of Archdeacon Robert Johnson who founded the school in 1584 adorns the Victoria Tower on the front of the school.

Bradgate Park
Snow covered much of Leicestershire at the time this photograph was taken, closing many schools,
and Bradgate Park was the ideal place to spend an unexpected day's holiday.

Abbey Park, Leicester

The red arms of the signpost create a focal point in this image. Lying just to the
north of the city centre, Leicester's most popular park was opened in 1882.

De Montfort Hall, Leicester

The hall is Leicester's main venue for concerts and has played host to famous artists such as Genesis, Blondie and Iron Maiden. Local favourite Engelbert Humperdinck has performed here on many occasions.

Robert Hall Statue, Leicester
Reverend Robert Hall was an influential Baptist minister. His statue stands in De Montfort Square,
adjacent to New Walk, a pedestrian thoroughfare which leads towards the city centre.

Jewry Wall, Leicester
The wall is part of Leicester's Roman baths and has survived for more than two thousand years.
The arched doorways are thought to have linked the gymnasium and the cold room.

Claybrooke Parva
An old wooden gate stands before St Peter's Church. These gates represent good photo
opportunities but are sadly being replaced across the rural landscape by the less attractive metal variety.

Bitteswell
The carpet of snow on the village green recedes as the February weather becomes milder.

East Norton
This small Leicestershire village lies in a valley beside the main A47 trunk road between
Leicester and Uppingham. A dusting of snow covers the hills in the distance.

Knighton Park, Leicester
Winter trees are lit up by late afternoon sunshine.

Orton on the Hill
The village lies to the far west of Leicestershire close to the Warwickshire border. This was the best display of snowdrops I encountered as I travelled around taking photos for this book.

St Wistan's Church, Wistow
Bare trees and a stormy sky create a stark, winter scene.

Clipsham Yew Tree Avenue, Rutland
Located beyond the A1, the Great North Road, this unique collection of clipped yew trees is so far east,
you would presume they were in Lincolnshire but they are actually still within the boundaries of Rutland.
Part of the Kesteven Forest, the trees are trimmed every autumn by Forestry Commission craftsmen.
For futher information visit www.forestry.gov.uk

The Buttercross, Hallaton
Hallaton is famous for its tradition of bottle kicking which is fought
out against the neighbouring village of Medbourne on Easter Monday.
Butter was once sold from the conical shaped buttercross on the village green.

St Giles Church, Medbourne
Medbourne is Hallaton's opponent in the bottle kicking event on Easter Monday.

Normanton, Rutland Water
Fishing boats moored at Normanton on Rutland water. Normanton Church,
Rutland's most famous landmark, is visible between the trees.

Manton, Rutland
This traditional, wooden signpost is located outside the village of Manton
on the road which runs along the southern shore of Rutland Water.

Broughton Astley
A small brook runs past St Mary's Church. Broughton Astley is the largest
village in Leicestershire and one of the largest villages in England.

Bosworth Battlefield
A stone monument marks the spot where Richard III, the Last Plantagenet
King of England, is said to have been killed during the Battle of Bosworth in 1485.

Swithland Woods
Footpaths crisscross between the trees and the lush green foliage of early spring.

Bluebells, Swithland Woods
A carpet of bluebells flourish in the shadows deep inside Swithland Woods.

Thornton Reservoir
The reservoir lies with the National Forest which is an environmental project to create a new forest
for the nation. The forest stretches between Leicestershire, Derbyshire and Staffordshire.

Sence Valley Forest Park

Also part of the National Forest, Sence Valley is situated close to the town of Ibstock. The area was previously an opencast mine and was opened to the public in 1998 after being planted with 98,000 trees.

Quorn

Previously called Quorndon, this village is associated with Leicestershire's tradition of foxhunting and lends its' name to the famous 'Quorn Hunt.' Note the fox on top of the thatched roof.

Rothley Station
A steam train waits to depart Rothley Station on the Great Central Railway.

Donington le Heath Manor House
This medieval manor house near Coalville is now a museum set within
recreated gardens. It is maintained by Leicestershire County Council.

Kirby Muxloe Castle
The imposing brick-built gatehouse of a largely uncompleted fortified manor house.
The moat completely surrounds this haunting ruin.

Sir Frank Whittle Memorial, Lutterworth
A model of Britain's first jet aircraft, the Gloster E28/39, stands as a memorial to Sir Frank Whittle who developed jet engines in Lutterworth at the beginning of the Second World War. The model stands in the middle of a roundabout to the south of the town.

Bust of Sir Frank Whittle, Lutterworth
A bust of Sir Frank Whittle stands in the centre of the market town. His right hand is placed on the jet engine he invented.

Suspension Bridge, Leicester
This footbridge crosses a section of the Grand Union Canal in Leicester and leads into Castle Gardens.

Liberty Statue, Leicester
This replica of the Statue of Liberty previously stood on top of the Liberty shoe factory on Eastern Boulevard. The factory was demolished in 2003 and the statue has been relocated to a roundabout on Upperton Road nearby.

River Soar, Abbey Park, Leicester
Trees in blossom line the River Soar as it passes through Abbey Park.

Abbey Park, Leicester
Colourful spring flowers brighten the park in early April.

Argents Mead, Hinckley
An octagonal bandstand shares Argents Mead with the offices of Hinckley and Bosworth Borough Council, opened in 1967.

Sheepy Magna
The close proximity of the Black Horse pub to All Saint's Church is captured in this photo.

Snibston Discovery Park, Coalville

Snibston Discovery Park is an interactive museum built on the site of a former colliery. The pithead which is a scheduled ancient monument can be seen from the town centre and serves as a reminder of the area's industrial heritage. The museum is administered by Leicestershire County Council.

The Clock Tower, Coalville
The clock tower in the middle of Coalville in northwest Leicestershire is the town's war memorial.

Tur Langton
The orb of the setting sun creates a silhouette of St Andrew's Church.

Market Bosworth
Shadows creep towards The Old Black Horse Inn as the sun descends on a glorious April evening.

Moira Furnace

Moira Furnace is an iron-making blast furnace located in Moira on the banks of a restored section of the Ashby Canal. It was built by the Earl of Moira in 1804.

Ashby de la Zouch
This half-timbered building on Market Street is now a charity shop and an entrance leads through to the Tudor Court Tearooms.

The Ashby Canal, Shackerstone
The marks on this picture are not dust spots on the lens but midges!

Market Bosworth
The distinctive architecture of the Dixie Grammar School and the
Bank Building are located in the market square of this rural town.

Castle View, Leicester
Fallen May blossom lies on the pavement along the cobbled street called Castle View. The spire of St Mary de Castro Church can be seen in the distance rising above the castle wall.

The Curve Theatre, Leicester
I needed to use a wide angle lens to capture the spectacular design of the new Curve Theatre
on Rutland Street. The building was designed by Rafael Vinoly and officially opened by the Queen.

Rearsby
The seven-arch packhorse bridge over Rearsby Brook is only a footbridge and traffic wishing
to cross the brook must use the ford which is on the other side of the bridge in this photo.

The River Wreake, Thrussington
The River Wreake and Holy Trinity Church under a cloudless April sky.

The River Wreake, Hoby
The footpath from Hoby to Rotherby crosses the River Wreake by way of this
old brick bridge. The village of Hoby can be seen to the right of the bridge.

The River Wreake, Hoby
Another shot of the River Wreake near Hoby as it meanders lazily through the trees. The spire of All Saints Church, Hoby is visible between the trees.

Grimston
The tractor, the wooden gate and the church tower are the key elements
of this rural scene on the approach to Grimston in north-east Leicestershire.

Wartnaby
A sea of yellow oilseed rape seems to isolate the village of Wartnaby.

River Soar, Mountsorrel
Water tumbles over a weir in this view of Mountsorrel and the River Soar. The war memorial can be seen
on top of Castle Hill and the tower of Saint Peter's Church, one of two Anglican churches in the village.

Millennium Mammoth, Watermead Country Park, Leicester
This model of a life size woolly mammoth stands on top of a hill overlooking
Watermead Country Park to the north of the city. Remains of such an animal were
found in the park confirming woolly mammoths roamed the area during the Ice Age.

Ashby Canal, Snarestone

One of the hidden gems of Leicestershire is the Ashby Canal at Snarestone. In fact it is so well hidden, it is buried and travels under the village through a tunnel! The tunnel is visible at the far end of the towpath.

Heather
May blossom dominates this view of Heather in the National Forest.

Waltham on the Wolds
The Marquis of Granby pub overlooks the village green in
Waltham on the Wolds to the north of Melton Mowbray.

Croxton Kerrial
This unusually named village lies close to the Lincolnshire border in north-east Leicestershire.

River Eye, Melton Mowbray
Egerton Park and the River Eye viewed from the bridge on Leicester Road.

St Mary's Church, Garthorpe
This scene of an English country church is enhanced by the bright
red post box and the fluffy white cloud. Garthorpe is close to the Lincolnshire
border and the tower of the church was built with Lincolnshire limestone.

Coston
The ford on the road between Coston and Sproxton

Saltby
An expanse of yellow oilseed rape creates a colourful approach to the village of Saltby.

Whissendine Windmill, Rutland
This seven storey windmill built in 1809 has been restored and is now producing flour again.

Wymondham
The Berkeley Arms public house on Main Street was built in 1692.

Loughborough from Beacon Hill
The town of Loughborough viewed between the crags at the summit of Beacon Hill. Towers Hall,
a hall of residence at Loughborough University, can be distinguished in the centre of the image.

Foxton Locks
Water cascades like a
waterfall as a boat descends
through the locks.

Hallaton
St Michael and All Angels Church commands a lofty position as the road winds into the village.

Horninghold

Situated close to the Rutland border, Horninghold must be a contender for one of Leicestershire's prettiest villages.

Uppingham, Rutland
The market place is still in shadow as the spire of St Peter and St Paul Church catches the early morning sun.

Eyebrook Reservoir
Eye Brook flows into the reservoir on the Leicestershire and Rutland border. The reservoir was built to supply water to the steelworks at Corby and was used during the Second World War by the RAF as they practised for the dambuster raids.

Groby Pool
The pool lies between Groby and Newtown Linford on the southern edge of Charnwood Forest.
There is some doubt as to whether the pool is a natural or a man-made lake. One theory suggests it
was dammed by monks from Leicester Abbey. Today the pool is a popular place to walk and feed ducks.

Beacon Hill

At 248 metres (815 feet) Beacon Hill is the second highest point in Leicestershire.
On a clear day, and with good eyesight you, can see Lincoln Cathedral!

Rainbow Bridge, Foxton
The surface of the Grand Union Union Canal mirrors the shape of the bridge on a still and idyllic July evening.

Medbourne
The garden of the Nevill Arms public house overlooks the brook as it runs
through the centre of the village and trips over a small waterfall.

Edith Weston, Rutland
Situated on the south shore of Rutland Water, the village is named
after Queen Edith of Wessex who married Edward the Confessor.

Rutland Water
Fly fishing is one of the many pursuits available at Rutland water
and the reservoir is said to be the best trout fishing venue in the UK.

St Andrew Church, Stoke Dry, Rutland
This small village overlooking Eyebrook Reservoir has links to the Gunpowder Plot. There are
claims the plotters met in a small room over the porch in the church but this has never been proven.
However, Sir Everard Digby whose family owned land in the parish was executed for his part in the plot.

Bede House, Lyddington, Rutland
Bede House was formerly a medieval palace belonging to the Bishops of Lincoln. It was subsequently converted into an almshouse and is now administered by English Heritage.

Hambleton, Rutland

Hambleton is the village in the middle of Rutland water and is surrounded on three sides by the reservoir. The land it is situated on is known as the Hambleton Peninsula.

Whitwell, Rutland Water
Yachts moored at Whitwell on the north shore of Rutland Water.

The *Rutland Belle*
The *Rutland Belle* is the boat which cruises around Rutland Water. Cruises
depart from Whitwell harbour with the option of visiting Normanton Church.

Normanton Church, Rutland Water
The church is Rutland's most iconic landmark. The proposed water line of Rutland Water would have flooded
the church so a trust was formed to save it. As a result, the level of the church was raised and protected by a pier of stones.
The church, previously called 'St Matthews', was deconsecrated in 1970 with the construction of the reservoir.

Kirby Muxloe Castle
A view of the castle from the far side of the moat. The castle is now maintained by
English Heritage and is open to the public during the summer months.

Leicester Cathedral
Located in the St Martins area of the city, Leicester Cathedral is one of the
smallest Anglican cathedrals in England. It became a cathedral in 1927.

Exton, Rutland
The Fox and Hounds pub stands on the far side of an idyllic village green shaded by mature trees.

St Helen's Church, Gumley
The cows in this picture look deceptively friendly but only a few moments earlier they had been stampeding towards me!
After I managed to calm them down and convince them they couldn't eat my camera, I got them to pose for me.

Thornton Reservoir
A lone fisherman enjoys the peace and solitude of the reservoir.